STRATEGIC STUDIES INSTITUTE

I0435641

The Strategic Studies Institute (SSI) is part of the U.S. Army War College and is the strategic-level study agent for issues related to national security and military strategy with emphasis on geostrategic analysis.

The mission of SSI is to use independent analysis to conduct strategic studies that develop policy recommendations on:

- Strategy, planning, and policy for joint and combined employment of military forces;

- Regional strategic appraisals;

- The nature of land warfare;

- Matters affecting the Army's future;

- The concepts, philosophy, and theory of strategy; and,

- Other issues of importance to the leadership of the Army.

Studies produced by civilian and military analysts concern topics having strategic implications for the Army, the Department of Defense, and the larger national security community.

In addition to its studies, SSI publishes special reports on topics of special or immediate interest. These include edited proceedings of conferences and topically oriented roundtables, expanded trip reports, and quick-reaction responses to senior Army leaders.

The Institute provides a valuable analytical capability within the Army to address strategic and other issues in support of Army participation in national security policy formulation.

i

The United States Army War College

The United States Army War College educates and develops leaders for service at the strategic level while advancing knowledge in the global application of Landpower.

The purpose of the United States Army War College is to produce graduates who are skilled critical thinkers and complex problem solvers. Concurrently, it is our duty to the U.S. Army to also act as a "think factory" for commanders and civilian leaders at the strategic level worldwide and routinely engage in discourse and debate concerning the role of ground forces in achieving national security objectives.

The Strategic Studies Institute publishes national security and strategic research and analysis to influence policy debate and bridge the gap between military and academia.

The Center for Strategic Leadership and Development contributes to the education of world class senior leaders, develops expert knowledge, and provides solutions to strategic Army issues affecting the national security community.

The Peacekeeping and Stability Operations Institute provides subject matter expertise, technical review, and writing expertise to agencies that develop stability operations concepts and doctrines.

The Senior Leader Development and Resiliency program supports the United States Army War College's lines of effort to educate strategic leaders and provide well-being education and support by developing self-awareness through leader feedback and leader resiliency.

The School of Strategic Landpower develops strategic leaders by providing a strong foundation of wisdom grounded in mastery of the profession of arms, and by serving as a crucible for educating future leaders in the analysis, evaluation, and refinement of professional expertise in war, strategy, operations, national security, resource management, and responsible command.

The U.S. Army Heritage and Education Center acquires, conserves, and exhibits historical materials for use to support the U.S. Army, educate an international audience, and honor Soldiers—past and present.

Strategic Studies Institute
and
U.S. Army War College Press

REVIVAL OF POLITICAL ISLAM IN THE AFTERMATH OF THE ARAB UPRISINGS: IMPLICATIONS FOR THE REGION AND BEYOND

Mohammed El-Katiri

July 2014

FOREWORD

Regime change during the Arab Spring allowed Islamist political forces that long had been marginalized to achieve political influence in Tunisia, Egypt, and Libya. Meanwhile, Morocco's first government led by an Islamist party has been in power since January 2012. This trend caused widespread concern over the future direction of these states; but despite the tragic example of Egypt, few negative predictions have yet been borne out.

In this monograph, Dr. El-Katiri, a British analyst with many years of experience in reporting on the Middle East and North Africa, cautions against an overly simplistic assessment of this rise in the influence and power of political Islam. He uses an extensive range of source material to show that the political crises besetting each of these Islamist governments are not necessarily of their own making, but instead are determined by objective circumstances. He also describes how in several key respects the aims of Islamist parties are in line with U.S. aspirations for the region.

The Strategic Studies Institute recommends this monograph to all readers studying and working with North African states, as well as those interested in the topic of political Islam more broadly.

DOUGLAS C. LOVELACE, JR.
Director
Strategic Studies Institute and
U.S. Army War College Press

ABOUT THE AUTHOR

MOHAMMED EL-KATIRI is a Director of MENA Insights, a political risk consultancy that focuses on the Middle East and North Africa, and a Senior Research Analyst at the United Kingdom's (UK) Conflict Studies Research Centre (CSRC). Before joining CSRC, Dr. El-Katiri was a Research Fellow at the UK Defence Academy, and later served as a Political Risk Analyst at Eurasia Group and as a senior researcher at the Hague Institute for Global Justice. He has more than 10 years of regional experience. His research interests include political and economic security in North Africa and the Gulf Cooperation Council (GCC) states, North African relations with the European Union, and security policies around the Mediterranean. Dr. El-Katiri has published numerous internal and external UK Defence Academy reports, including reference papers on national and regional security issues in the GCC and the Mediterranean and a monograph on the Algerian national oil and gas company Sonatrach. His publications also include commentaries and research papers in a range of languages for research organizations in the UK and Europe, as well as various newspaper articles dealing with the region. Dr. El-Katiri is a frequent commentator in media, including the BBC, the *Financial Times*, and *Al-Jazeera*.

SUMMARY

As part of the radical political changes that have affected a number of Arab countries over the past 4 years, the toppling of regimes and the organization of the first fair and free elections in several Arab states have allowed Islamist parties to rise to power. This highly visible political trend has caused mixed reactions, both within these countries and internationally. Prior to the Arab Spring, most countries in the region banned Islamist movements from forming political parties. For decades, members of such movements were jailed, tortured, and exiled from their home countries. Even in those states where Islamist political parties were allowed, they had limited freedom and were under the scrutiny of the regimes, as was, for example, the Moroccan Justice and Development Party.

The varied experiences of Islamist political parties in power over the last 2 years in Tunisia, Morocco, and Egypt offer a mixed picture. The debacle of Muslim Brotherhood rule in Egypt captured a great deal of international attention, but it did not resemble the trajectory of other governing Islamist parties in the region. Electorates have been disappointed by the performance of Islamist-led governments, which turned out to be unprepared to govern. Their poor performance is not only due to a lack of capability; it is also due to the fact that integration into the existing political system has not been smooth and free of obstruction. Islamist parties have faced fierce resistance both from secular parties and other forces in their respective societies and from abroad, as is evident from the opposition of rich Arab Gulf Monarchies.

Completed in 2013, this monograph does not include the most recent political developments in all of the three countries under discussion, but it establishes a number of important and persistent themes. It provides an overview of the factors behind the victory of Islamist parties in Egypt, Morocco, and Tunisia, and continues by examining their performance in power in different policy areas, with a particular focus on foreign policy. It argues that policymakers should not follow the popular trend of reducing the delicate political transition underway in Egypt, Tunisia, and Morocco to simple ideological differences between Islamist parties and their secular opponents. Instead, this is a reflection of an ongoing struggle between traditional elites. Furthermore, it should be remembered that, contrary to widespread fears, the foreign policy aims of Islamist political parties in North Africa coincide with the aims of the United States and its allies in a number of key areas.

REVIVAL OF POLITICAL ISLAM IN THE AFTERMATH OF THE ARAB UPRISINGS: IMPLICATIONS FOR THE REGION AND BEYOND

INTRODUCTION

The uprisings that have swept across the Arab world since December 2010 have resulted in drastic changes in the political landscape of several countries, and brought new dynamics in intraregional relations. The long-term political regimes first of Tunisia, then Egypt, Libya, and later Yemen were ousted, and other Arab leaders were pressured to announce a set of institutional and constitutional reforms. Subsequent elections for new governments brought about sweeping victories for Islamic parties in both Tunisia and Egypt, with Islamic protest movements crowding the streets in many other Arab neighbors, including Libya, Algeria, and Syria. Morocco's first government led by an Islamic party took office in January 2012, following increasingly large electoral successes at two previous elections in the 2000s. These victories are no small development for the Arab region; for the first time in the modern history of these countries, Islamic political parties are now ascending to power through democratic elections.

Islamist groups do not have to win elections to change the political landscape; the experiences of Algeria and Libya provide instructive examples. Against the expectations of many observers, Islamists performed poorly in the 2012 elections in both countries, but they continue to distort local politics. In Libya, a victory by liberals does not mean the influence of Islamists in the political sphere has vanished. The Muslim Brotherhood-inspired Islamist group is shaping the political and security situation in parliament and the streets through its militias. In Algeria, the Islamist parties were not victorious in the legislative elections of May 2012, a result that surprised many observers who predicted Algeria would follow in the footsteps of its neighbors, Morocco and Tunisia. But Algeria's election results have generated much discussion within Algerian political circles about the role of the regime in manipulating the elections.[1]

Where Islamic governments are already in power in the Islamic world, their troubles are not over. At the time of this writing, the three elected Islamist governments in the region are each experiencing a political crisis that has either suspended their rule or threatens their coalitions. In Egypt, the Egyptian military ousted President Mohammed Morsi in July 2013 and arrested several of his ministers and leaders of the Muslim Brotherhood. In Tunisia and Morocco, both Islamist-led governments are entangled in political crises that may cause their coalition governments to fall apart.

The problems these governments face are not necessarily self-inflicted. Both in Egypt and in Tunisia, and to some extent also in Morocco, Islamist parties came to power at the most challenging political and economic moment since these countries gained independence decades ago. They inherited precarious and challenging economic situations, characterized by widening budget deficits, soaring food prices, dwindling foreign reserves, and increased unemployment. Facing these enormous challenges, the Arab world's Islamist parties share a common lack of governing experience, often tied to (1) their first time in office; (2) their typically high focus on religious-ideological topics rather than core themes such as economic reform beyond broad welfarist rhetoric; and (3) in many cases an election result that surprised their political leaders themselves. Simply put, they were not prepared to govern.

Entirely separate from the old internecine ties that in the past characterized Arab political regimes, the Arab world's Islamist parties lack the culture of bureaucratic clientelism that characterized the de facto single-party systems in Tunisia and Egypt, and Morocco's varying ruling coalitions of palace-trusted parties since the 1960s. Being part of a larger coalition has not helped these parties integrate particularly well into their national political context; they seem, rather, detached from these coalitions, neither learning from more experienced coalition partners, nor being able to put forward those supposed policies that were meant to govern their own political programs. The apparent outcome appears for the most part to be one of stalled Islamist politics, that have produced few of the results their supporters initially endorsed.

In this monograph, we endeavor not to give a survey of all political Islam-inspired groups in the Middle East, but instead to focus on moderate Islamist parties that are in power or (as was the case of Egypt) have led coalition governments, and to review their behavior and agenda in the current changing and challenging circumstances of the Middle East and North Africa. The monograph is primarily concerned with the performance of Islamist-led governments over the 2 years to 2013, with particular focus on the approach to the three countries' foreign relations. Despite their various socio-economic, historical, and political realities, and an ideological orientation that markedly set apart the Islamist government of Morocco from those of Tunisia and Egypt, the three face a set of commonalities, including a complicated political backdrop and lack of experience in running a government. For this analysis, we highlight common features that characterize the time in power of all these governments, leading to conclusions about the nature of political Islam as a whole.

The first section of the monograph examines the reasons behind the Islamist parties emerging as the main political force in the first free and fair elections in the history of the region. The second section outlines the internal political and economic challenges faced by these Islamist-led governments over the previous 2 years. Finally, the third section discusses the trajectory of the three countries' foreign policies during the Islamists' rule.

FOUNDATIONS OF ISLAMIST ELECTORAL SUCCESS

To gauge the importance of the moderate Islamists' ascent to power, a brief history of their political experience is necessary. In contrast to many radical Islamic groups that believed in and adopted violence as a way to achieve political change, moderate Islamist movements adopted a more constructive attitude and role in society. They rejected violence and accepted democratic rules as a way to compete for political power, including as political parties. During the 1990s and 2000s, many of these groups, including the Egyptian Muslim Brotherhood, gradually turned into de facto opposition movements, using human rights and democratic rhetoric and the fight against systemic corruption in existing political cadres as an integral part of their political programs.[2] Throughout the years, many of these groups managed to refine and moderate their political thinking and win more support across society.

Morocco's Party of Justice and Development (PJD), Tunisia's Ennahda movement, and Egypt's Muslim Brotherhood have since pragmatically moderated their stances on several societal issues such as personal liberties, gender equality, and economic affairs. In the Moroccan and Tunisian case, women have been a critical element, both within those parties and as supporters and voters. The PJD party has promoted itself as a very moderate Islamic party, dissipating fears among some that the party could turn into another Algerian Islamic Salvation Front; the party embraces through its rhetoric human rights and the importance of tourism, and has shied away from including views about the consumption of alcohol in its program. Within government, the party has focused on social sector reform, rather than on ministries traditionally held and managed by the King or one of his allied parties, such as the Ministry of Finance and the Ministry of Islamic Affairs.

The bloody outcome of the Arab world's first electoral victory of an Islamic party, the Islamic Salvation Front (FIS) in Algeria in 1991, nevertheless served as a first warning to those who seemed to believe that the future of the Middle East could be assured under Islamic-democratic governments. The victory of FIS in the first round of elections led to the military moving in to cancel the second round in December 1991, which led to the outbreak of a decade-long civil war and is estimated to have cost 200,000 lives. Although the Islamist movements were an influential political force, their political participation thereafter was restrained. The Islamist movements were not allowed to form political parties and participate formally in elections, and so, in most countries, members of Islamist movements would run for elections as independents.

Nevertheless, Islamic parties' discourses and activities constituted a serious challenge to the stability and continuity of political regimes in power in their respective countries. The Arab regimes observed with great concern the rise of Islamist movements, and used a range of measures to curb their progress and popularity among the public. Experiences varied from one country to another, but Islamists were prohibited from participating in political institutions as political parties for years and saw their members jailed, killed, or exiled. Even when Islamists were allowed to form a civil, not religious, political party, as was the case of PJD in Morocco,[3] they were deeply mistrusted and continuously scrutinized. The regimes used all communication tools and means to limit the moderate Islamists' appeal to the public. In Morocco, the rise to prominence of any Islamic movement is perceived as a challenge to exclusive prerogatives of the King. The Moroccan monarch, as Commander of the Faithful, is the supreme religious authority in the country. This spiritual position constitutes an important element of the monarch's legitimacy as a descendent of the prophet Mohammed. The Islamic movement in Tunisia suffered from oppression and persecutions for decades under Ben Ali's regime. Tunisian authorities rejected applications by Islamist movements to constitute a political party and participate in political life as an organization. Following the 1989 elections, most Ennahda leaders left the country to seek refuge in different countries around the world. Zine El Abidine Ben Ali's regime saw in the Islamists a threat to secularism and the interests of the ruling class.[4]

The experience in Egypt was not much different. The Muslim Brotherhood leadership and members were intimidated and harassed by the ruling party and security agencies.[5] Influential members of the Brotherhood organization were routinely arrested and sentenced to jail.[6] After they were outlawed in 1954 during Gamal Abdel Nasser's rule, Muslim Brotherhood members were banned from constituting a political party. They were only allowed to participate in legislative or local elections as independent candidates during Mubarak's rule, but with a tacit agreement that they should present a limited number of independent candidates.

The post-revolution era saw a change of approach toward the Islamist movements' aspirations to participate in the political system. Several political parties have been legalized in Egypt, Libya, and Tunisia. In Egypt, the Al-Nour party, representing the Salafi movement, was legalized in June 2011 by the Political Parties Affairs Commission,[7] and became the second most important political party in the country. In the same period, the Muslim Brotherhood received a favorable response to its demand to establish the Freedom and Justice Party. Post-Qadhafi Libya saw the burgeoning of political parties after revoking a law introduced by Qadhafi in the 1970s that banned political parties, including the Islamist Justice and Construction party and Al-Umma al-Wasat party. Another movement that came to prominence in revolution-affected countries is the Salafi groups in Tunisia, Egypt, and Morocco.

It is only with this background in mind that one can understand the momentousness of the change in the Arab political landscape. But the question remains of how the Islamists garnered all the support they needed for landslide victories. The triumph of Islamists in elections can be attributed to two main factors. First, the popularity of these parties is mainly accredited to the fact that millions of Arabs see in Islamist politicians an answer to their socio-economic expectations. High rates of unemployment, soaring living costs, and regional and social income disparities were some of the fundamental factors that sparked protests and revolutions across the region since December 2010.[8] These were the kind of issues that Islamist movements have striven to address. Moderate Islamist groups capitalized on all the failures and shortcomings of previous governments in order to build their political discourse.

The Islamist parties campaigned to fight corruption and bring fair distribution of wealth; they have opposed regimes' oppressive and undemocratic practices; they called for respect for human rights and the need to introduce democratic reforms and good governance; in many cases, they strengthened their credibility by matching their words with actions, by building schools and hospitals, and by collecting money for various social causes. For years, Islamic movements in all countries played an important role in providing services that the state failed to provide to economically and socially marginalized social groups. The Muslim Brotherhood in Egypt, for instance, ran charitable organizations, schools, hospitals, and housing cooperatives for millions of Egyptians.[9] It provided loans to start businesses for entrepreneurs. This made the movements very popular among many disenfranchised social groups and political idealists (educated groups that dreamed of a well-functioning, fair, and democratic nation) in Arab societies. Moreover, both membership and the constituency of Islamist parties differs significantly from that of other established parties: these are not based on family, tribal, ethnic, or other long-term established clientelist ties, but rather on a shared belief. In Morocco, Egypt, and Tunisia, where few sectarian minorities exist, the popular feeling of "we," versus the old-established system of "them" ruling "us," is perhaps best captured by the Islamist movements—a factor explaining the mass appeal of these movements.

Second, the collapse of the dominant ruling parties in Egypt and Tunisia—the National Democratic Party and *Rassemblement Constitutionnele Democratique* (RCD), alongside their long-term presidents, Hosni Mubarak and Zineddine Ben Ali, respectively—left a vacuum in the political scene. Having dominated political life in its entirety for decades, these parties left few other options in the political playing field. With both systemic and popular pressure for a quick handover of power via new elections, little time was available for the development of political culture and parties, leaving the field open to those social trends with the most established support—which, under these totalitarian regimes, were the primary socially active Islamic networks. Other opposition parties were small and weak. Their failure to win large public support has been ascribed to several factors, chief among them being weak leadership, lack of internal democracy and detachment from the masses' demands and aspirations.[10] Often including former members of the ousted regimes, they were perceived as regime-endorsed parties lacking any genuine interest in bringing about political and economic changes. On the contrary, the moderate Islamists managed to gain the reputation of being genuine in their opposition to the regime and calls for rotation of power—many of them had themselves been harassed and imprisoned for many years and therefore held credibility in their aspiration for change. In Morocco, a country that was not so much affected by the popular upheavals, the traditional leftist political parties lost their popular political appeal after their poor performance in previous governments since the 1990s.

Political Islam emerged as the main winner of the popular upheavals and revolutions that swept the Arab world since December 2010, despite the fact that the Islamist movement had no leadership role in the instigation of popular protests. The triumph of Islamist parties has been a historical turning point in the political history of these Arab countries. It might not have been entirely surprising for countries like Egypt and Morocco, where Islamists had large constituencies and a history of participation in the political life, but their victory in Tunisia was unexpected and surprised Tunisian political and civil society as well as the outside world. In Egypt, the Muslim Brotherhood had been the only challenging force to the ruling National Democratic Party (NDP) in parliamentary elections since 2000. In 2005, the Muslim Brotherhood, through its members presenting as independent candidates, won 88 seats in the Egyptian parliament despite still at that point being a banned organization.[11]

Alarmed by the rise of this movement, the Egyptian regime responded with the adoption of a set of measures to restrain the Islamist organization's role in the political institutions.[12] Measures employed by the Egyptian regime included arrests of Muslim Brotherhood members, including some of its leading figures, and closures of businesses owned by Muslim Brotherhood members. These measures, coupled with manipulation of votes and voters, resulted in dramatic losses of Muslim Brotherhood candidates in the 2010 parliamentary elections, and a landslide victory for the NDP. Meanwhile in Morocco, PJD had been licensed as political party since the mid-1990s, participating actively in Moroccan political life since then. Over the next 2 decades, PJD strengthened its position in the Moroccan political scene, and the number of parliament seats won by its candidates grew steadily since its first participation in general elections in 1997.

THE END OF THE HONEYMOON:
THE MANY CHALLENGES FACING
THE ISLAMIST GOVERNMENTS

Translating the initial momentum of electoral support into real policy change in the region has not been an easy task for the elected Islamists. The Islamist-led governments had to deal with many urgent issues, chief among them inherited socio-economic problems that had been much exacerbated in Tunisia and Egypt by months of political upheaval, legal and economic uncertainty, and a national security service at high political alert. Moreover, as newcomers to the political system, Islamist parties have generally faced the challenge of how to integrate and function on a political level surrounded by the remnants of the old regimes which are still very much present. The revolutions in Egypt and Tunisia deposed key figures of the political systems but did not remove the bureaucracy and, most importantly, did not eradicate old mindsets. The old regime was composed of security officers, bureaucrats, judiciary officials, and businessmen that had vested interests in the continuity and the stability of the system. In Morocco, many parts of the bureaucracy, including ministerial staff, are the predominant clients of the *Makhzen*, the ruling establishment made up of the King and his supporters, including Palace-supported political parties. In this context, it becomes less surprising that Islamist politics have not yet found an effective path forward.

Integrating New Parties into Old Political Structures.

The rise to prominence of Islamist parties in several Arab countries was not welcomed by all segments of Arab societies and ruling regimes. For instance, the elected Islamists encountered stiff resistance from the bureaucratic apparatus. Several bureaucratic elites, who in theory are supposed to be politically neutral, showed strong antipathy toward the Islamists and their reform agenda. Several instances of tensions have emerged between Islamists and civil service institutions. Bureaucrats have blocked or delayed procedures or were not responsive to the governmental initiatives. Senior technocrats appointed by the former regimes in Egypt and Tunisia, or by the King in Morocco, have aligned their forces with leftist parties, secularism proponents, and economic elites in order to oppose the Islamists. The power struggle between the judiciary and Egypt's Morsi on several reform projects is an illustration of the difficulties the Islamist rulers have faced.[13]

It should be noted that the opposition of bureaucracy cadres was not only ideologically driven, but in most cases is a struggle to maintain power, privileges, and economic interests. Many proponents of Islam from the regimes are socially conservative, but still would not support an Islamist reform agenda. Morocco is the best example where many influential families that make up the *Makhzen* are conservative, and adherence to Islamic values and traditions constitutes a significant part of their social prestige. Nevertheless, they are still considered opponents of PJD and its socio-economic reform agenda. In sum, bureaucratic opposition is not oriented solely against Islamists but against any political formation that could endanger existing socio-economic entitlements.

This resistance was expected. Most technocrats were part of a culture that perceived Islam-inspired political movements as an existential threat to the regimes of which they were a part. These technocrats played an important role in government strategies to manage the phenomenon of political Islam. Responses by previous regimes ranged from repression to co-option approaches, from persecuting and jailing the Islamist militants and activists to allowing them to run for elections. Unlike Libya, where the post-revolution government adopted a vetting law that affected officers and officials from across the state bureaucracy, Tunisia and Egypt have taken a different course. In Tunisia, the draft "law for the protection of the revolution" is not as broad as the Libyan one. Vetting has been limited to senior political figures who served in Ben Ali's government or the dissolved Constitutional Democratic Rally (CDR).[14]

The Islamist-led coalition governments in Tunisia and Morocco have gone through episodes of tensions between Islamist parties on one hand, and their government partners and opposition parties on the other.[15] This is more pronounced in the case of Tunisia, where secular resistance to the Islamist government triggered social unrest and political revolt for months in Tunisian cities, and plunged the country into political uncertainty. Residents of Sidi Bouzid, a town where the revolution began in December 2010, took to the streets on several occasions to protest against the failure of the Islamist-led government to tackle their socio-economic grievances. Some of these protests lead to violent confrontations with police forces, as was the case in August 2012.[16] Similar violent protests happened in other peripheral cities such as the protests in Siliana in November 2012.[17] The protests were not only confined to the peripheral cities, but have also affected the capital Tunis that experienced several riots and strikes. In June 2012, the Tunisian government imposed an overnight curfew following violent protests by Salafists over an art exhibition that was deemed disrespectful of Islamic morality.[18]

The difficult political transition almost fractured the Ennahda party in February 2013. Islamist Prime Minister Hamadi Jebali proposed without any consultation with his party a plan to form an apolitical government. This attempt to appease the political tensions and polarization of Tunisian society was worsened further by the assassination of leftist political leader Chokri Belaid, and ensuing violent protests. The solution did not win political support within Ennahda and was fiercely rejected by several key members of the party, including its leader, Rachid Ghannoushi, on the basis of concerns regarding the image and credibility of the party in front of its voters.

Following his failure to form a government of technocrats, Jebali resigned from his position.[19] A new cabinet was formed where important ministerial portfolios, such as defense, interior, and justice, went to technocrats. These political concessions did not win Ennahda peace. Unsatisfied about limited political power to shape the new political order in the post-Ben Ali era, the secular opposition parties have constantly criticized the performance of the Ennahda-led government. Secular critics have accused Ennahda of adopting a lax attitude toward increasing Salafi violence, and of having a hidden counterdemocratic agenda. These accusations and counteraccusations between the two political blocs have polarized Tunisian society still further. In the view of Tunisian intellectuals, this emerging schism poses the main security threat to Tunisian society, and could push the country to chaos.[20] After months of political standstill, the Ennahda party has at the time of this writing still not reached an agreement with the secular opposition parties to end their political differences and agree on a political road map.[21] The opposition parties are calling for the dissolution of the current government and the holding of new elections.

Morocco remained relatively stable compared to Egypt and Tunisia. The country did not experience mass violence, and most demonstrations were peaceful. However, the government still went through continuous political crises. At the time of this writing, the PJD-led government is on the brink of collapse. Since its election victory in 2011, PJD's ministers and decisions had received continuous criticism from opposition parties, in particular from its ideological rival, the Authenticity and Modernity Party. This group is regarded by many observers as the Palace's party, and one of its fundamental missions since its establishment in 2008 has been to limit the political dominance of Islamist movements. The antagonism toward the PJD ministers was not limited to its opposition rivals but came also from within its coalition partners. The PJD-led government became a minority government following the withdrawal of one of its important coalition partners, the Istiqlal Party, in June 2013. The PJD had no other options than to approach one of its opposition rivals, the National Rally of Independents, to negotiate the terms of their participation in the government.[22] The Moroccan electoral system does not allow any party to win a clear majority and govern alone.

Islamists also have external opponents. Several countries have seen in the rise of Islamist parties a direct threat to their strategic interests. At the regional level, the Gulf monarchies saw in the election of the Muslim Brotherhood in Egypt a threat to their own national stability and interests in the region. Historically, Egyptian Muslim Brothers have had an influence on their offshoots across the Arab world, including in the Gulf countries. The Gulf rulers were concerned that these ties could be exploited to challenge their authority. United Arab Emirates (UAE) Foreign Minister, Abdullah bin Zayed, openly expressed these concerns, saying that:

> The Muslim Brotherhood does not believe in the nation state. It does not believe in the sovereignty of the state. There were individuals within the Muslim Brotherhood who would be able to use their prestige and capabilities to violate the sovereignty, laws and rules of other countries.[23]

Based on these assumptions, Gulf regimes, led by Saudi Arabia and the UAE, worked actively to restrain the political success of the Muslim Brotherhood during the period of Morsi's rule. Gulf countries, other than Qatar, froze their financial aid to Egypt in order to accentuate the failure of the Islamists. It is revealing that both Saudi Arabia and the UAE announced $8 billion in aid to tackle Egypt's immediate financial and economic problems directly after the ousting of Morsi.[24] The timing of the Gulf rulers' generosity was aimed to send a strong signal to Egyptian voters that voting against the Muslim Brotherhood brings prosperity.[25]

Beyond the Arab world, a statement by French Minister of the Interior Manuel Valls illustrates such fears. He remarked that:

> There is an Islamic fascism rising everywhere, but this obscurantism must, of course, be condemned because it denies the democracy for which the Libyan, Tunisian and Egyptian people have fought... it is a considerable issue... not only for Tunisians but for the whole Mediterranean space and thus for France.[26]

Ideological Opposition of Secularists and Religious Minorities.

This change in the political balance has alarmed religious and political forces and minorities, particularly secularist parties, which saw in these developments a potential threat to liberal and modern values and, most importantly, to their privileges. These concerns are not new.

Liberals and secularists have a history of resentment against Islamists in the Arab world. The victory of Islamists in several Arab countries revived old disagreements and rivalry between Islamists and secularists. The general concern of the liberal and secularist groups is the future of civil liberties and freedoms. For instance, the rise of the Muslim Brotherhood after the 2005 parliamentary elections worried Copts and leftists in Egypt because of the potential influence that the Brotherhood could exercise on legislation. The vagueness of the Muslim Brotherhood's societal project remains the primary contributor to the worries of Egyptian minorities and liberals. The long-standing slogan, "Islam is the solution," used by the Muslim Brothers in many parliamentary elections is confusing and adds to the anxiety of the proponents of a civil state. In effect, the Muslim Brotherhood has failed to explain how exactly Islam will provide solutions to Egypt's problems. A comment by a Coptic intellectual published in the Egyptian newspaper, *Al-Ahram,* captures the worries of his community once the Muslim Brotherhood is in power, "rich Copts will leave the country while the poor Copts will stay . . . maybe some of them will be converted . . . I hope I die before this happens."[27]

The return of sectarian strife across different Egyptian regions since the ousting of Mubarak has reinforced worries among Copts. Although the Muslim Brotherhood apparently did not incite its members to attack Copts, the involvement of Islamists in attacks against Copts or justification of such clashes on a religious basis have only entrenched the idea that Islamists are a threat to the Copts.

The ongoing political discussion in post-revolution Egypt on the role of Islam as a source of legislation is another important illustration of the divide between the two groups. Attempts by Egyptian and Tunisian Islamists in constituent assemblies to give Islam and Islamic law an important position in the constitutions draw strong opposition from secularist groups and parties that advocate a separation between religion and politics.

During the electoral campaigns, most Islamist public figures in Morocco, Tunisia, and Egypt were pushed, by inflammatory media articles and protests, to reassure the public about their adherence to democratic rules, and respect for human rights and personal liberties as well as a free market. They had to clarify their positions to local public and international observers on different issues including tourism, consumption of alcohol, the role of women in society, and that it is not their intention to impose a way of life or make people more religious. In an article published in the British newspaper, *The Guardian*, Tunisia's Rachid Ghannouchi wrote that:

> We have long advocated democracy within the mainstream trend of political Islam, which we feel is the best system that protects against injustice and authoritarianism. In addition, it provides institutions and mechanisms to guarantee personal and public liberties . . . protection of the rights of women, separation of powers, independence of the judiciary, press and media freedom and protection of minority rights. All these are in no way contradictory with Islam, but reflect the Islamic principles of consultation, justice and accountability as we understand them.[28]

The worries of secularists and non-Muslim minorities might appear exaggerated. But there are precedents in Gaza and Iran, where Islamist governments adopted a range of policy initiatives to "moralize" their respective societies.[29] The mistrust runs so deep between the two groups that attempts by Islamist leaders in Morocco and Tunisia to display moderation and pragmatism in their political and societal plans have only brought limited success. Originally, this schism was an ideological disagreement limited to intellectuals, but secularism has come to serve as a symbol of protection of the interests of the political and economic elites, including figures from the old regimes in the case of Tunisia and Egypt.

Insufficient Institutional Capability.

Elected governments in Tunisia and Egypt inherited a murky economic situation following the revolutions in January 2011. The price of the revolutions was economic recession, increased unemployment, and severe imbalances in public finances. Political instability and uncertainty have severely affected the functioning of key economic sectors in both countries. For example, continuous strikes and social unrest have hampered phosphate production in Ghafsa, Tunisia, and phosphate accounts for 7 percent of Tunisian gross domestic product (GDP). In 2012, the Compagnie des Phosphates de Ghafsa lost 60 percent of its production compared to previous years.[30] Tourist arrivals in both countries have, unsurprisingly, dropped significantly over the last 3 years, and have failed to return to pre-revolution levels. Both countries have lost their attractiveness to foreign investors. Foreign Direct Investments (FDI) have dropped considerably.[31]

Thus, it is not surprising that addressing economic challenges featured in political discourses and government decisions as the first priority of the Islamist-led governments in the region. Their focus started with restoring macroeconomic stability, but since then has not moved on from this approach. Their reforms were not aimed at solving structural economic issues such as unemployment, inflation, and stimulating economic growth, but rather focused on tackling fiscal stability and foreign reserves. They lacked a comprehensive plan to deal with the difficult economic challenges of their respective societies. With no exception, all the Islamist-led governments have failed to come up with comprehensive and sustainable policy initiatives to stimulate economic growth, create jobs, and attract investments. The Islamist-led governments were mainly in a reactive rather than a proactive mode.

It is not only foreign investors that were deterred by social and political tensions and uncertainty, but also local investors. Consumer and business confidence have been considerably weakened since the eruption of protests and upheavals in Tunisia and Egypt. Political and legal uncertainties remain the key factors that are discouraging domestic investors to invest their capital in the local economy. For households, it is uncertainty about their jobs and continuity of their income that limits their consumption behavior.

Some government decisions have further contributed to business community worries. For instance, judicial investigations on corruption cases involving businesses linked to the ousted Ben Ali clan have not finished, and they are maintaining a high state of anxiety among the Tunisian business community. Hundreds of Tunisian businessmen are banned from travelling abroad.[32] The decision of the Egyptian Islamist government to launch a tax-evasion investigation against one of the most influential business families, the Sawiris, was a strategic error and a shortsighted decision. The case ended with a financial settlement[33] but did not erase the concerns of the Egyptian business community about the future steps of the government. The community saw in this case a precedent that could be further pursued by the government against many crony-capitalists from the Mubarak era.

Another initiative that has alarmed both the secular and traditional business community was the launch of the Egyptian Business Development Association by the Muslim Brotherhood's business elites. The most important rationale for the new business association was to counter the influence of the existing powerful Mubarak-linked businessmen, and provide the government with ideas for its economic policy decisions. The establishment of this new business association that mainly groups business owners who are sympathetic with Islamist political goals and ideals, was perceived by Egyptian economic elites as a signal of the Muslim Brotherhood's ambitions to replicate the strategy of the governing Turkish Islamist party, the Justice and Development Party (AKP), in challenging their economic interests and political power.[34] The "Islamic Bourgeoisie," referring to the Anatolian entrepreneurs, is considered the backbone of the AKP's economic and political success.[35]

In Egypt, the Islamist government encountered difficulties in its negotiations with international financial institutions to get loans for its development projects. Lack of agreement after onerous and lengthy negotiations between the International Monetary Fund (IMF) and the Egyptian government has negatively impacted the Egyptian economy, particularly its credit rating in international markets. Disagreement on IMF conditionality for a $4.8 billion loan sends alarming messages about the future growth and macroeconomic stability of Egypt. IMF economic adjustment requirements to add new taxes and reduce spending on subsidies have been regarded by the Egyptian government as not the most sensible approach given post-revolution political and economic conditions. The Egyptian authorities do not disagree on the need for reform to bring more efficiency in the way fuel and food subsidies are spent, but they object to the timing with which these reforms should be implemented. The Egyptian government judges immediate implementation to be inappropriate given the country's political climate and people's expectations.

Over and above the technical details, political divisions and instability have complicated the negotiation of a financial loan deal. The IMF has required a consensus among key political forces on the reform program in the country in order to ensure its application over the coming years, which has been impossible to achieve given the severe political disagreement among different political forces in the government and opposition.

The Islamist movements were caught off guard by the unexpected change of the political scene in their respective countries, as was any other political force in the region and international community as a whole. The Islamist movements were simply not ready to rule. This is understandable in the case of the Ennahda in Tunisia, relatively new to political participation. But the cases of the Muslim Brotherhood in Egypt and, more importantly, the Moroccan PJD evidence a failure to prepare to govern. Both organizations had been very active in local politics for decades. For instance, PJD had been established as a political party for almost 20 years, had participated in a number of legislative and local elections, and played a leading role in the parliamentary opposition. But it had invested little in preparing to govern the country.

The economic challenges that Egypt, Morocco, and Tunisia are currently experiencing, with varying degrees of severity, are another symptom of the unpreparedness of the Islamists to govern. Socioeconomic indicators have deteriorated.[36] The main reason is the lack of business experience and expertise of the Islamist leaders and among their cadres. The second reason is more political in nature. The Islamists lacked the political instinct to counter the maneuvering of their opponents from the traditional economic and political elites and their established patronage network that extended into the public administration.

The problems of Islamist movements have not been lack of knowledgeable individuals on economic affairs, but rather lack of institutions and teams that are able to develop strategies for key sectors and implement them. Some of these individuals had theoretical knowledge that was not accompanied with practical expertise to bring real change on the ground. For instance, Ridha Saidi, Ennahda's leading economist, had showed an understanding of the needs of some of the country's strategic economic sectors during the electoral campaign in 2011, such as the tourism sector, and promised several steps to revitalize the industry.[37] The suggested solutions were a series of generic common sense measures, which did not reflect any innovative thinking to present a tailor-made solution that tackled the structural problems of the sector or recognize the ongoing political instability and lack of security.

What all the Islamist parties that achieved power have lacked is the support of an advisory group of experts that are able to provide policy-oriented advice and prepare initiatives to the government. The Islamists relied entirely on the technocrats in the bureaucracy to develop new initiatives to present to the government for endorsement and implementation. This has been a naïve assumption and a tactical mistake. The governing Islamist leadership did not take into consideration the lack of capacity — and willingness — of the executive cadres to provide such solutions.

Although socio-economic reforms were at the center of their demands and concerns, Islamist parties never developed alternative policies or thinking to achieve economic growth and improve economic conditions for the majority. This structural dearth of governing experience and policy implementation capability was evident in the electoral campaigns. The Islamist parties' manifestos lacked any detailed economic sections on how to deal with the economic challenges. Apart from generic aims such as fighting corruption and building an economy based on solidarity and Islamic values, the programs did not include any specific measures and instruments on how to attain such goals.

The Islamist parties failed to benefit from several meetings with the business community during the electoral campaign to develop a strategic vision to achieve economic growth. Their objective, then, was primarily aimed at reassuring investors of their commitments to market economy and support for investments. For instance, the Ennahda leadership had meetings with different Tunisian business organizations in the country. In November 2011, Ennahda organized a conference on the tourism sector to discuss with private sector investors ways and means to develop the sector, but only limited practical steps have followed. The Islamist-led government plan, announced by the Islamist Prime Minister Abdelilah Benkirane in January 2012 at the Moroccan parliament, did not include any details on how the government is aiming to achieve macro-economic balances and create job opportunities. The document did not include a single detailed policy on how to reduce the budget deficit or reform tax policy.[38]

ISLAMIST FOREIGN POLICY: A PRAGMATIC TRAJECTORY

The momentous change in the political landscape of the three countries has not led to significant policy change in their external relations. Foreign policy did not feature as a priority policy area for the Islamist-led governments, with their concern and discourse focusing instead on internal political and socio-economic issues. During the electoral campaign, the discourses focused mainly on themes and policies with broad appeal to masses—jobs, fighting corruption, and cronyism. References to foreign relation issues were brief and aimed at signaling continuity to international investors and to governments of strategic importance. There has been no document released that outlines the key objectives of foreign policy, or the priorities for today and the coming years.

Conversely, foreign observers have shown much interest in the position of these much-feared political players in international affairs. The arrival of Islamists in power in Egypt, Morocco, and Tunisia raised questions about how the foreign policy of each country and of the entire region would develop. For many observers, the immediate concern was relations with Israel and the Western world. For instance, would Egypt revoke its peace agreement with Israel? Would there be a radical change of policy stance toward the Israeli-Palestinian conflict? Would security cooperation between the United States and its Arab Mediterranean partners continue or experience difficulties? Would changes of government imply a transfiguration of the region's strategic relations with emerging global powers? For a country like France, the dramatic changes in the political landscape sowed doubts in politicians' and strategists' minds about the future of their strategic presence in the North African countries.

Two years of Islamist rule in Morocco and Tunisia brought no shift in the focus and interests of foreign policy of either country. This continuity is attributed to several key factors. First, the Islamist movements never had a grand strategy for foreign policy. Thus, their arrival to power did not lead to any major changes in their governments' foreign policy stances and choices. The pragmatism that has characterized Moroccan and Tunisian diplomacy still dominates the thinking and practice of the foreign policy cadres. Foreign policy was mainly designed to protect national economic and political interests, and not to follow any ideological value or rhetoric such as pan-Arabism or liberal democracy. In the case of Morocco, core national political interests merely refer to preserving the national unity and territorial integrity of the country vis-à-vis Western Sahara and the Spanish enclaves in the North of Morocco. The country's leadership opted for a low profile policy on regional and international political affairs. The hegemonic aspirations of Morocco in the Maghreb have been muted. The Moroccan leadership refrains from openly playing a leading role in regional affairs at this critical geostrategic juncture.

The stance of Tunisia regarding the French military intervention in Mali is characteristic of the pragmatism adopted by the Islamists in foreign policy. In January 2013 Tunisian Foreign Minister Rafik Abdessalem voiced sympathy with the French intervention against the terrorist groups in northern regions of Mali.[39] This showed that strategic relations with France outweigh the idealistic perspectives of the political party.

Second, the change of the political landscape in Tunisia and Morocco did not result in a change of bureaucracy. The technocrats and civil servants remained in their positions. In Tunisia, diplomats were not at the center of public scrutiny. The Foreign Affairs Ministry was not strongly associated with the wrongdoings of Ben Ali's regime in the same way as the Ministry of Interior. For most Tunisians, it was mainly city governors and senior members of the dominant ruling party, CDR, that were seen as remnants of Ben Ali loyalists. In Morocco, the foreign policy of the country is to a large extent a domain of the royal palace. The newly-endorsed constitution of July 2011, which primarily aimed to placate street protests, has brought no change to the palace's dominant role in driving Morocco's diplomatic relations. The appointment of former Foreign minister Taib Fassi Fehri as the King's advisor, and Yousef Amrani as minister delegate at the Foreign Ministry next to the Islamist Minister, Saadeddin Othmani, was intended both to signal and to assure the continuity of the palace's dominance in shaping the foreign policy of Morocco. This has been clear to most of Morocco's partners, and led to less deep concern than in the cases of Tunisia or Egypt.

Third, Islamists have sensed that the imperatives of social stability and economic growth would have to drive foreign policy priorities. Relations with Western governments are perceived as the route to a prosperous economy. Both countries are economically dependent on their relations with European countries. France remains the largest trading partner of Tunisia and Morocco. Tunisia's new leaders capitalized on the political change that is taking place in their country to request from their European peers a reinforcement of their partnership. In November 2012, Tunisia was granted the status of "advanced partner," which aims to further reduce barriers to free movement of goods, services, and people.[40] In Morocco, strengthening strategic relations with the European continent featured in the discourse and initiatives of the PJD-led government.

In Egypt, the election of Islamists inaugurated a new era for the country's external relations. Changes have been few, but remarkable. The most important ones are related to Egypt's relations with Israel. The two countries have enjoyed relatively stable security relations since the signing of the peace treaty in 1979. But the ousting of Mubarak's government and Egypt's ongoing turbulent transition brought new challenges for Israel. The concerns of Israeli policymakers about the stability of their country's relations with Egypt were not misguided.[41] There were moments of tensions between the two countries following the ousting of Mubarak and during the rule of the Supreme Council of Armed Forces (SCAF), a military junta that ruled Egypt from January 2011 until July 2012, and the Muslim Brotherhood. The Egyptian-Israeli "gas trade diplomacy" was the first to suffer the repercussions of political change in Egypt. Recurring attacks on the gas pipelines resulted in a prolonged disruption of gas supplies to Israel in 2011.[42] The targeting of this strategic infrastructure was not random. The gas trade between the two countries has been a controversial issue since the signing of the agreement in 2005. Members of Egyptian civil society campaigned for years to cancel the deal on a commercial basis.[43] Under pressure of public opinion, the Egyptian authorities first announced their intention to review the prices of their gas exported to Israel.[44] In April 2012, Egypt announced a unilateral termination of its gas supply contract to Israel. Egyptian authorities asserted that the cancelation was due to domestic shortages and not to political motives.

Egypt recalled its Ambassador in Tel Aviv, Israel, twice, once under the military rule, and the second time at the decision of Morsi's government to protest Israeli strikes on the Gaza strip.[45] It is important to note that Egypt's post-revolution rulers showed pragmatism in managing their delicate relations with Israel, far from any ideological or nationalist dogma. The only factor that drove the Egyptian rulers was public opinion, and both the military and the Muslim Brotherhood avoided being deemed complacent toward Israel. Meanwhile, Egypt's rulers have tried hard to convey a message of continuity in their diplomatic relations with Israel, and that their commitment to honoring the Camp David Accords with Israel remains a fundamental pillar of Egyptian foreign policy.

At the same time, precarious political and economic circumstances have forced Egypt's leadership to freeze their ambitions to play a leadership role in the Middle East. For decades, Egypt was regarded as the central regional power with its large army and dynamic diplomacy. But the mediation of Morsi in the 2012 Israel-Gaza conflict should be seen more as motivated by domestic Egyptian factors. An escalation of the conflict on Egypt's borders could have put the Muslim Brotherhood in a difficult position, given the long relations between the Brotherhood and Hamas and delicate relations with Israel.[46]

The limited rapprochement with Iran remains the most controversial foreign policy episode of President Morsi's time in government. The exchange of visits between the two heads of state provoked concerns among Egypt's traditional strategic partners, the United States, Gulf Cooperation Council (GCC) countries, and Israel, about the future direction of Egypt's international relations agenda. Morsi's initiative did more harm to the image of Egypt by confusing its strategic neighbors. U.S. and GCC policymakers saw in this rapprochement by one of their most important security allies an attempt to undermine their efforts to isolate Iran and pressure its political elites to reconsider their nuclear development plans. Distancing itself from Iran constituted an important element of the previous government's cooperation framework with the GCC. Over the previous decade, GCC countries, particularly Saudi Arabia, had established a doctrine in their relations with Arab and Muslim countries vis-à-vis the Iranian threat that could be summarized as "you are either with us or with the other."

The exchange of visits between Iranian President Mahmoud Ahmadinejad and Egyptian President Mohamed Morsi was not regarded merely as a routine protocol exercise. It was rather a continuation of years of contacts and mutual admiration. The ties between the Egyptian Muslim Brotherhood and Iran predate the Arab Spring, despite their ideological differences. In 2009, Mohammed Mahdi Akef, ex-Supreme Guide of the Muslim Brotherhood, confirmed this contact with the Iranians in an interview published on Al-jazeera's website, and explained the position of the Muslim Brotherhood vis-à-vis the interaction with Iran despite sectarian rivalry. As a Sunni organization, he asserted that the Muslim Brotherhood deals with the Iranian state, and not with Shi'ism as sect.[47] But most importantly, Muslim Brotherhood leaders have seen in the Iranian Islamic government a practical embodiment of their political ideals to establish an Islamic state.

Critical voices also emerged from within President Morsi's circle of collaborators. Fouad Jabblah, ex-legal advisor to Morsi who resigned in 2013, warned the

Islamist-led government in an interview published in the pan-Arab newspaper, Asharq al-Awsat, of the damage that the rapprochement with Iran is causing to Egypt's national interests, particularly with the Gulf rulers.[48] Iran is no replacement for GCC countries: There is a limit of what Iran, with its own economic difficulties, can offer to Egyptians. The GCC countries, in contrast, provide millions of employment opportunities to Egyptian families. Wealthy GCC countries provide economic assistance and are a source of inward investment in the Egyptian economy.

This shift in Egypt's foreign relations with its strategic partners might have cheered ordinary people, but certainly did not enjoy the full backing of all Egyptian institutions. The Egyptian military, a key beneficiary of the peace agreement with Israel through U.S. military aid, was alarmed about the degradation of Egypt's relations with Israel. They observed how anxious Israeli leaders were about the obscure direction of Egyptian foreign policy interests and the country's stability. Deteriorating relations with Israel would come at a high price. The U.S. aid has been tacitly part of the Camp David peace package, aimed at strengthening the interest of Egypt in keeping the peace agreement.

Military officers rarely make any public statements on Egypt's relation with Israel. But through recent decades, senior military officers have had good relations with their counterparts in Israel. The quality of these relations could be deduced from the positions adopted by Israeli diplomats and politicians, who lobbied in Washington and across western capitals in favor of military control of power in Egypt. After the ousting of Morsi in July 2012, Israel openly called on the United States to maintain its aid package.[49]

There has been a palpable sense of urgency among policymakers to strengthen Arab regional cooperation and integration. In North Africa, leaders confronted with ongoing protests and acknowledging the common socio-economic challenges facing their countries saw reactivation of an economic integration project as a pertinent policy measure to reduce the risks of instability. But so far, there has been limited success. Politicians in transition countries naturally prioritize political and security issues over strengthening regional integration. Furthermore, the same geopolitical hurdles that impeded the Maghreb Arab Union project for decades remain unresolved. Animosity and mistrust between Algeria and Morocco prevail. Land borders have remained closed between the two countries since 1994, and recent attempts to negotiate a reopening have yielded no results.

Ironically, it is the opposite that is happening. The fragile political and security situations in Tunisia, Libya, and Egypt have had a negative impact on a range of planned and existing economic integration projects. Egyptian gas exports to Jordan and other neighboring countries, for example, have suffered from disruptions as a result of repeated bombings of Sinai pipelines.

Turkey has seen a window of opportunity opening with the Arab Spring revolution, to strengthen its position in the Middle East. In line with its soft power strategy to win the hearts and minds of the Arab people over the last decade, the Turkish leadership has aligned with demands to establish democratic regimes and respect human rights. Turkish Prime Minister Recep Tayyip Erdogan sided with protestors and asked Mubarak to relinquish power.[50] The AKP political brand appeals to Islamist movements in the region. The Turkish model was perceived a successful model of a modern and prosperous state run by an Islamic government. The Turkish democratic experience is seen as the most relevant example to Arab socio-cultural realities. The AKP's skillful strategy to contain the political and economic influence of secular elites has been appreciated by Islamist governments in the Arab world. Turkey is used as a case study because of spectacular economic performance since AKP came to power.

To win strategic and long-term friendships in the region, the Turkish leadership was proactive in providing Islamic political parties with logistical support and strategic guidance. This element of AKP foreign policy doctrine was spelled out by Kemal Dervis, Turkey's ex-Minister of Economic Affairs, who noted that "friendships in the new world are more important than membership of various clubs- including the European Union."[51] Turkey's interests are not solely ideological, but rather serve to achieve an economic foothold in these North African countries. The frequency of visits is a strong indicator of the importance of the relationship between Turkey and these countries. Istanbul and Ankara became important destinations for Islamist political leaders mainly from Libya, Tunisia, and Egypt. Erdogan, accompanied by Turkish industrialists and businessmen, has paid visits to all North African countries with the aim of strengthening his government's and Turkey's political and economic ties with the region.[52]

CONCLUSIONS AND POLICY IMPLICATIONS

Since the fall of the regimes in Egypt and Tunisia in January 2011, the political scene in the region has seen major transformations; new political parties have been formed, several free and, by most accounts, reasonably fair elections have been organized, and a new cadre of political parties—many of them with Islamic voices—have acquired government positions in three Arab countries. The victory of Islamists sparked fears and uncertainty within the countries and beyond. Domestically, secular and religious minorities have been concerned about the future of their individual rights and religious freedoms. At the regional level, neighboring countries have feared that the rise of Islamist parties, particularly the Muslim Brotherhood in Egypt, could be mirrored by similar transformation in their own territories.

To various degrees this scenario remains of concern for the Arab world's republics, most of which already face an explicit or covert Islamic opposition; as well as for its monarchies, particularly those of the Gulf in which political parties so far do not yet exist, and for whom transnational organizations such as the Egyptian Muslim Brotherhood present a potentially threatening scenario if transplanted into their own national contexts. In the West, much of the worry is focused on how Islamist domestic and foreign policies are going to impact the geopolitics of the Middle East and North Africa region and whether those potential future Islamist-led governments will ever forge the kind of political ties the long-held Mubarak and Ben Ali regimes held with the West, despite their internally largely undemocratic natures.

However, it seems that these worries have not translated into the worst case scenarios put forward by those opposing the inclusion of Islamist parties in Middle East politics *a priori*. In the case of Morocco and Tunisia, Islamist leaders have displayed some moderation and—seemingly—pragmatism in their domestic political and societal plans as well as in managing their governments' external relations. Neither in Morocco, nor in Tunisia, have Islamist parties so far attempted, nor shown the institutional capacity, to change fundamentally the way their national political systems are run—be this in a positive or negative sense. The Islamist-led governments of both countries have at best disappointed many of their voters' expectations for real change. This may indeed be a lesson with a value of its own, in a region where Islamist electoral victories have often been accompanied by huge positive or negative expectations.

In Egypt, the Muslim Brotherhood experience was different. Decisively more deconstructive, the Muslim Brotherhood's rule was, in many ways, too short to allow for any realistic long-term positive outcome, but the damage it did to the "image" of Islamist rule both in Egypt and the wider region is undeniably negative. The multifaceted relationship between the Muslim Brotherhood on the one hand, and its more Salafist coalition partners on the other, with various foreign governments and political orientations, including Iran, Saudi Arabia, Qatar, Hamas, and various Palestinian factions, as well as the party's troubled relationship with its own domestic security forces and the military, imply that the problem in Egypt is significantly more complex, and cannot be reduced only to the "failure" of one particular political stream. Instead, it is a telling episode about the difficulty of reconstructing and rebuilding political systems according to parameters which remain unclear—such as the role of religion under constitutional law, and the intended content of policymaking beyond vague ideas of "social justice" and the "fight against corruption and the former regime."

Nevertheless, all three experiences have to various degrees demonstrated that despite their apparent vast popularity amongst the Arab street masses, the Arab world's Islamist parties have not been prepared to govern. They lacked the structures and qualified human resources to handle affairs of state. It has been easy for the Islamist leaders, while in opposition or in exile, to criticize previous governments and the regimes behind them, highlighting their incompetence or lack of integrity. Once in office, Islamist politicians have themselves been confronted with the challenging reality of taking responsibility to manage the nation's affairs. All the Islamist governments in the region have failed to handle political and economic challenges. They have been unsuccessful in stabilizing the economy in countries affected by revolution or tackling the unemployment issue. Almost 2 years after the coming to power of the first Islamist government in the region, no alternative economic policy initiative has yet been put forward.

But despite these structural limitations and meager progress in reform, Islamists still retain substantial public support. Regardless that the reputation of Islamists has suffered significant damage, particularly in Egypt, as result of public disillusionment with limited reforms the chance of Islamists of winning new elections remains high. This is especially the case if the current coalition governments fail to work with their partners or the opposition, a scenario that is likely to happen given the ongoing political standoffs in Tunisia and Morocco. Currently, there is still a lack of strong and credible political parties in the countries that could provide an alternative cohesive plan that wins the support of large number of voters.

The problem remains not Islamic ideology and values *per se*, but the general lack of experience, and skill, of these parties to translate these values into realistic, sensible policies. Only the development of this capability could turn Islamist parties into the sort of force at work politically in many European countries, for instance Christian Democrats and other parties, whose aim is to translate economic and legal reform into social benefit based on traditional social and religious values. In the absence of any such realization within the Arab world's Islamist parties, their role will likely continue to be one of an opposition movement, with no ideas of their own other than ideological ones, and no realistic long-term role in rebuilding, rather than deconstructing economies and political systems.

The difficult political situation that has characterized these three countries over recent years will remain in place for a prolonged period. Significant political reforms are not going to be easily implemented. The Islamist parties in Tunisia and Morocco still have to face a lengthy confrontation with the cronies and bureaucracy of Ben Ali and the Moroccan Palace. Every reform initiative will have to navigate its way through different stages of resistance from parliament, bureaucracy, and the business community. In Egypt, after the military ousting of elected president Morsi, the country has entered a new phase in its political transition that is going to be characterized by further insecurity and political instability. The disagreement between supporters of the deposed Muslim Brotherhood president and his opponents will not fade away peacefully or soon. What is happening in Egypt is a manifestation of an emerging political phenomenon that is likely to characterize the wider Arab region, whereby Arab societies are becoming more and more polarized between secularists and Islamists. This is already having a negative impact on the political stability and security of Arab countries as a whole.

One key lesson to draw from these years of political tumult is that building a stable democracy is an evolutionary process and takes time. It is not an affair of quick wins or a zero-sum game. It is a diligent exercise that requires inclusion, dialogue, compromise, and a forward-looking mindset. Governing a transition without a compromise is counterintuitive and makes it difficult for these countries to move forward. Rebuilding a country, even holding elections in the absence of common social agreement over its format and tools, will be difficult within an electoral process, with or without Islamist forces. The enormously emotive debate surrounding proposed constitutional changes by Egypt's Muslim Brotherhood-led government after the elections is an important illustrating point—such constitutional issues should have been resolved long before any elected government had taken up its role.

Lastly, any successful transition will require the contribution of civil society and its role in keeping the public expectations at reasonable levels. Dealing with the wide socio-economic problems the Arab world is facing is a task that has been beyond consecutive established governments and the international community for many decades. The outbreak of political unrest is merely the tip of the iceberg of long-held frustration and aggression against any form of political regime. No new government, whether Islamist-led or not, could be expected to rectify decades of problems within a year or two; meaning that one of the most valuable assets these governments will need is time and stability. It is difficult for the Islamists to negotiate with their political adversaries while their positions are driven by idealistic political expectations; and it will be difficult for them to reform any part of the political system, without knowledge, skill, and realistic goals and tools in their hands.

Policy Implications.

- U.S. policymakers should not follow the popular trend of reducing the delicate political transition underway in Egypt, Tunisia, and Morocco to simple ideological differences between Islamist parties and their secular opponents. Instead, it is a reflection of an ongoing struggle between traditional elites that have benefited economically and politically from the political system of previous decades, and the new political forces that seek gradual change toward more transparency and accountability. In this respect, the aims of Islamist aspirations are in line with U.S. aspirations for the region.
- Furthermore, the coming to power of moderate Islamist governments in countries of the region does not automatically imply a deterioration of relations with the United States and its allies. In the three examples under consideration, pragmatism in foreign policy has prevailed.
- Meanwhile, for as long as Arab countries lack stable governments and an inclusive political environment that is based on compromise and dialogue, the region remains susceptible to further instability. The inability of these governments to meet the expectations and demands of their people is likely to lead to more popular protest and unrest. These countries' fragile socio-economic situations render them vulner-

able to fluctuations in global economic growth and changes in the prices of international commodities. Further upheaval should be expected and prepared for.

- It is therefore important for the U.S. Government to continue playing its important role in stabilizing the region through the provision of a range of financial, educational, military, and diplomatic support. It is critical for the success of the ongoing political transitions that there should be more emphasis on enhancing the capabilities of the current Arab governments, officials, and institutions in various policy areas. At the same time, government officials and institutions are not the only important actors requiring support; there should be more engagement with political parties, civil society. and the private sector. Building a new political system is essential, and this cannot be other than a joint effort of all societal structures and of individuals.

- There remains a vital role for the U.S. military, both in direct assistance and in training and education for these countries' armed forces. Education in post-conflict state building, leveraging U.S. lessons from the last 2 decades of conflicts and troubled transitions, should be emphasized, as well as continuing essential efforts toward security sector reform and providing best-practice guidance in civil-military relations, regardless of who is leading the government. Security and defense institutions have proved to be less susceptible to Islamist ideological influences. This will foster the creation of more stable societies in the target countries during and after this process of political change.

- The United States and the international community should prioritize the promotion of comprehensive dialogue among all social groups and communities in these societies characterized by a multitude of ethnic, religious, and ideological groups. National dialogue is the most effective instrument to shorten transitions to new political eras, and should be assisted wherever possible.

ENDNOTES

1. Arezki Daoud, "Legislative Elections: Algeria Takes Three-Steps Backward," *The North Africa Journal*, May 14, 2012, available from *www.north-africa.com/premium/opinions/2012/05/14/legislative-elections-algeria-takes-three-steps-backward/*.

2. Robert S. Leiken and Steven Brooke, "The Moderate Muslim Brotherhood," *Foreign Affairs*, Vol. 86, No. 2, March-April 2007, pp, 107-121.

3. The Moroccan political parties' law prohibits the formation of any party on a religious, ethnic, or regional basis. Thus, the Moroccan Justice and Development party prefers to describe itself as a political entity with Islamic references.

4. Khalid Elgindy, "The Rhetoric of Rachid Ghannushi," *The Arab Studies Journal*, Vol. 3, No. 1, 1995, pp. 101-119.

5. Mohamed A. El-Khawas, "Revolutionary Islam in North Africa: Challenges and Responses," *Africa Today*, Vol. 43, No. 4, October-December 1996, pp. 385-404.

6. Hesham Al-Awadi, *In Pursuit of Legitimacy: The Muslim Brothers and Mubarak, 1982-2000*, New York: Tauris Studies, 2004, p. 215.

7. "Al-Nour Party: Egypt's Salafis Go Maintream," *Asharq al-Awsat*, June 20, 2011, available from *www.aawsat.net/2011/06/article55246084*.

8. Beatrice Hibou, "La Tunisie en Revolution," ("Tunisia in Revolution"), *Politique Africaine*, No. 121, March 2011, pp. 5-22.

9. Noha Antar, "The Muslim Brotherhood's Success in the Legislative Elections in Egypt 2005: Reasons and Implications," *EuroMesco*, October 2006, pp. 15-16.

10. Amr Hamzawy, "Opposition in Egypt: Performance in the Presidential Election and Prospects for the Parliamentary Elections," *Policy Outlook*, Washington, DC: Carnegie Endowment for International Peace, October 2005, available from *carnegieendowment.org/files/PO22.hamzawy.FINAL.pdf*.

11. Ashraf Swelam, "Egypt's 2010 Parliamentary Elections: The Landslide," *Egypt's International Economic Forum*, January 2, 2011.

12. "Egypt's Muslim Brothers: Confrontation or Integration?" Middle East/North Africa Report No. 76, Brussels, Belgium: International Crisis Group, June 18, 2008.

13. Heba Saleh, "Riots Highlight Limits on Morsi's Power," *Financial Times*, January 31, 2013, available from *www.ft.com/cms/s/0/5bbbf4ee-6af2-11e2-9871-00144feab49a.html#axzz2eaLJ4WUs*.

14. Isabelle Mandraud, "En Tunisie, une loi prévoit d'exclure de la vie politique les anciens soutiens de Ben Ali," ("In Tunisia a Law Provides for the Exclusion of Former Supporters of Ben Ali from Political Life"), *Le Monde*, June 29, 2013, available from *www.lemonde.fr/international/article/2013/06/29/en-tunisie-une-loi-prevoit-d-exclure-de-la-vie-politique-les-anciens-soutiens-de-ben-ali_3438916_3210.html*.

15. Following its victory in the election of October 2011, the Tunisian Islamist party, Ennahda, formed a coalition with two leftist parties that traditionally opposed the Ben Ali regime, Congress pour la Republique (CPR) and Etakatoul (The Democratic Forum for Labor and Liberties).

16. Christopher Barrie, "Tunisia: Al-Nahda's Failures Lead Sidi Bouzide to Rise again," *Alakhbar* English, August 17, 2012, available from *english.al-akhbar.com/node/11211*.

17. "Tunisia: Riot Police Fire Birdshots at Protestors," Human Rights Watch, December 1, 2013, available from *www.hrw.org/news/2012/12/01/tunisia-riot-police-fire-birdshot-protesters*.

18. Borzou Daragahi, "Tunisia Restores Tense Calm after Riots," *Financial Times*, June 13, 2012, available from *www.ft.com/cms/s/0/8f4a050c-b527-11e1-ab92-00144feabdc0.html#axzz2laaObnYl*.

19. Arezki Daoud, "Tunisian PM Jebali Resigns: a case of "Should I Stay or Should I Go," *The North Africa Journal*, February 18, 2013, available from *www.north-africa.com/social_polics/security_politics/1febtwenty48.html*.

20. Interviews conducted by the author with Tunisian diplomats in The Hague, The Netherlands, April 2013.

21. Walid Khefifi, "Crise Politique: L'impass," ("Political Crisis: Impass"), *Le Temps*, August 25, 2013, available from *www.letemps.com.tn/article-78352.html*.

22. Benjamine Rogers, "Maroc: Crise Governementale, quelle solution pour le PJD?" ("Morocco: Governmental Crisis, which solution for the PJD?"), *Jeune Afrique*, July 12, 2013, available from *www.jeuneafrique.com/Article/ARTJAWEB20130712112038/*.

23. Ola Salem, "UAE Foreign Minister Urges Syria Action saying Arab League was Ignored," *The National*, October 9, 2012, available from *www.thenational.ae/news/uae-news/uae-foreign-minister-urges-syria-action-saying-arab-league-was-ignored*.

24. Bassem Aly, "Old Friends Never Die: Egyptian-Gulf Relations after Morsi," *Ahram* Online, July 14, 2013, available from *english.ahram.org.eg/News/76430.aspx*.

25. Michael Peel, Camilla Hall, and Heba Saleh, "Saudi Arabia and UAE Prop up Egypt Regime with Offer of $8bn," *Financial Times*, July 10, 2013, available from *www.ft.com/cms/s/0/7e066bdc-e8a2-11e2-8e9e-00144feabdc0.html#axzz2eP4Wj1sF*.

26. Joseph Byron, "French Minister Denounces 'Islamic Fascism Rising Everywhere' after Tunisia Killing of Anti-Islamist Politician," *European Jewish Press*, February 10, 2013, available from *eajc.org/page32/news36339.html*.

27. Amira Howeidy, "Who's Afraid of the Brotherhood?" *Al-Ahram Weekly* Online, Issue No. 70, November 24-30, 2005, available from *weekly.ahram.org.eg/2005/770/fr2.htm*.

28. Rachid Ghannouchi, "A Day to Inspire All Tunisians-Whether Islamic or Secular," *The Guardian*, October 17, 2011, available from *www.guardian.co.uk/commentisfree/2011/oct/17/tunisians-islamic-secular-ennahda-election*.

29. Mkhaimar Abusada, "Hamas and the Social Islamization of Gaza," *Bitterlemons International*, November 4, 2010, Ed. 21, available from *www.bitterlemons-international.org/inside.php?id=1312*. See also Abeer Ayyoub, "Hamas Pushes Islamization of Gaza," *Al-Monitor*, February 4, 2013, available from *www.al-monitor.com/pulse/originals/2013/02/hamas-islamization-gaza.html*.

30. "La Production du phosphate a Ghafsa enregistre une forte baisse au titre de l'annee 2012" ("Phosphate Production in Ghafsa Recorded a Sharp Decrease During 2012 Year"), *L'economist Maghrebin*, January 8, 2013, available from *www.leconomistemaghrebin.com/2013/01/08/la-production-du-phosphate-a-gafsa-enregistre-une-forte-baisse-au-titre-de-lannee-2012/*.

31. *World Economic Outlook: Hopes, Realities and Risks*, Washington, DC: International Monetary Fund (IMF), April 2013.

32. "Tunisia: Problem of 460 Businessmen Banned from Travel to be Solved in a few Weeks," *Africa Manager*, available from *www.africanmanager.com/site_eng/detail_article.php?art_id=17928*.

33. Sherine Abdel-Razek, "Sawiris Return," *Al-Ahram Weekly*, May 7, 2013, available from *weekly.ahram.org.eg/News/2505/18/Sawiris-returns.aspx*.

34. Borzou Draghi, "A New Voice for Egyptian Business," *Financial Times*, November 8, 2012, available from *www.ft.com/cms/s/0/a9509002-28ee-11e2-b92c-00144feabdc0.html#axzz2ZDvBy2zG*.

35. Hakan Yavuz, *Secularism and Muslim Democracy in Turkey*, Cambridge, UK: Cambridge University Press, 2009.

36. "Regional Economic Outlook Update: May 2013," Washington, DC: Middle East and Central Asia Department, IMF, available from *www.imf.org/external/pubs/ft/reo/2013/mcd/eng/pdf/mena-cca-stats.pdf.*

37. Redi Hamdi, "Le tourisme vu par Ennahda : paroles en l'air ou paroles sincères?" ("Tourism seen by Ennahda: lip service or sincere promises?"), *Destination Tunisie*, November 14, 2011, available from *www.destinationtunisie.info/le-tourisme-vu-par-ennahda-paroles-en-laeair-ou-paroles-sinca%C2%A8res/.*

38. "Al-barnmaj Al Hokomi" ("Moroccan Government's Plan"), Rabat, Morocco: Prime Minister Office, January 2013, available from *www.assdae.com/IMG/pdf/programme-gouvernement-benkirane-2012.pdf.*

39. Noureddin Hlaoui, "La Tunisie subit l'intervention française au Mali, la diplomatie flotte . . ." ("Tunisia affected by French Intervention in Mali, diplomacy fleet"), *Business News*, January 17, 2013, available from *www.businessnews.com.tn/La-Tunisie-subit-l'intervention-française-au-Mali,-la-diplomatie-flotte…,519,35750,1.*

40. "EU-Tunisia Association council," Press/12/479, Brussels, Belgium: Council of the European Union, November 12, 2012, available from *europa.eu/rapid/press-release_PRES-12-479_en.htm.*

41. Aluf Benn, "Mubarak's Departure Thwarted Israeli Strike on Iran," *Haaretz*, February 13, 2011, available from *www.haaretz.com/print-edition/news/mubarak-s-departure-thwarted-israeli-strike-on-iran-1.343012.*

42. "Financial Report 2012," Haifa, Israel: The Israel Electricity Company, available from *www.iec.co.il/EN/IR/Documents/December%202012.pdf.*

43. Mona Al-Naggar, "Court in Egypt Annuls Deal with Israel on Gas Supply," *The New York Times*, November 18, 2013, available from *www.nytimes.com/2008/11/19/world/middleeast/19egypt.html?_r=0.*

44. "EMG: Egypt Should Honor Israel Natgas Deal," *Egyptian Oil and Gas*, Issue 52, April 2011, available from *www.egyptoil-gas.com/admin/industry/News%20EOG%20Newspaper%20April%20 2011%20Issue.pdf*.

45. Raphael Ahren, "Protesting Israel's Gaza Operation, Egypt Withdraws Ambassador from Tel Aviv," *The Times of Israel*, November, 14, 2012, available from *www.timesofisrael.com/protesting-israels-gaza-operation-egypt-to-withdraw-ambassador-from-tel-aviv/*.

46. Roula Khalaf and Heba Saleh, "Morsi Praised for Role in Gaza Crisis," *Financial Times*, November 22, 2012, available from *www.ft.com/cms/s/0/db1c443a-34c1-11e2-99df-00144feabdc0.html# axzz2eP4Wj1sF*.

47. Today's Meeting Programme, "Mohammed Mahdi Akef . . . Muslim Brotherhood in Egypt," *Aljazeera*, April 10, 2009, available from *www.aljazeera.net/programs/pages/ca363af8-030f-4f2a-b6f7 -100a7a65ffab*.

48. "Fouad Jadallah: There are concerns about the appointment of a strong head of government to compete with the presidency role," *aawsat.com*, available on *aawsat.com/details.asp?section =4&article=726899&issueno=12574#.Uf5e0OChBFI*.

49. Chemi Shalev, "Sympathy for the Devil: Israel's Efforts on behalf of Cairo's Generals," *Haaretz*, August 20, 2013, available from *www.haaretz.com/blogs/west-of-eden/.premium-1.542403*.

50. Thomas Seibert, "Turkey's Erdogan Says Mubarak Should go Now," *The National*, February 3, 2011, available from *www. thenational.ae/news/world/middle-east/turkeys-erdogan-says-mubarak-should-go-now*.

51. Delphine Strauss, "New Assertiveness on the World Stage," *Financial Times*, June 28, 2013, available from *www. ft.com/cms/s/0/1aadc9a2-7fe8-11df-91b4-00144feabdc0.html#axzz 2dAmzznrM*.

52. Rania Abouzeid, "Why Turkey's Erdogan is Greeted like a Rock Star in Egypt" *Time*, September 13, 2011, available from *content.time.com/time/world/article/0,8599,2093090,00.html*; Sinem Sengiz, "Erdogan's North Africa Visit to Bolster Turkey's Africa Initiative," *Todays Zaman*, June 3, 2013, available from *www.todayszaman.com/news-317305-erdogans-north-africa-visit-to-bolster-turkeys-africa-initiative.html*.

U.S. ARMY WAR COLLEGE

Major General William E. Rapp
Commandant

*****

STRATEGIC STUDIES INSTITUTE
and
U.S. ARMY WAR COLLEGE PRESS

Director
Professor Douglas C. Lovelace, Jr.

Director of Research
Dr. Steven K. Metz

Author
Dr. Mohammed El-Katiri

Editor for Production
Dr. James G. Pierce

Publications Assistant
Ms. Rita A. Rummel

*****

Composition
Mrs. Jennifer E. Nevil